The Everything Bagel

@F.O.R.T.Y. for everyone
Copyright © 2021

Scottt Raven

The Everything Bagel

at this point i seem to have written about everything,
well, almost everything,
everything except everything itself

1. Almost Everything

contains all of existence on its ring shaped,
boiled then baked, flowy and doughy, circular surface,
boiled in every river, every lake,
inside every ocean of preconceived notions,
bathed in a basin of hatred and devotion
with the faithful and the faithless,
the furies and the fates
steamed, baked and carbon dated,
it's cooling contents
mingled with the extinct, endangered
and overpopulated

it's nothing to everyone and everything
to those with nothing to eat
an impossibly possible burgerless burger
of beyond beyond meat
meeting in the beyond
beyond the beyond and beyond the beyond beyond
this infinity tire of inspired, unexpired silk
freshly served with fat-free,
oat, soy, whole milk,
coconut, macadamia and walnut
at break fasts and fast breaks,
to wedding party guests and at wakes
to funeral attendees
borrowers, *Lenders*, by *Thomas'* and *Sarah Lees*
from *Udi's* gluten free to frozen *Maccabees-*
even as bite-sized treats with tomato sauce and cheese
on *Pepperidge Farms*, *L'oven Fresh*,
Daily Chef and *David Delis*

for those at business luncheons and corporate functions
in suits and dungarees,
with smoked salmon, creamy avocados and by hungry bees
for 5k, 10k and marathon racers,
at *Einstein Bros*, bodegas and fundraisers

not just garlic, salt, onions and poppy seeds,
but covered in hopes and dream cheese,
failures and triumphs,
curds, whey, butter, margarine, pb&j,
lox, stocks and barrels of monkeys,
money, honey and ice cream--
really, all toppings, spices,
accoutrements and condiments,

sure there's a few innocuous antioxidants,
but also scant traces of toxic waste,
cinnamon-swirled into infinite,
limitless,
lemony space

because as is the case
with everything,
everything good also comes along with
everything bad,
everything mediocre and everything in between,
everything seen and unseen,
the invisible, the visceral, the poisonous and medicinal,
death caps, red caps and milk caps,
truffles, wood ears
and the most magic
of mushrooms

there's also blueberries, raspberries,
strawberries, bilberries,
acai berries, cranberries,
grapes and gojis,

all graphics, hieroglyphs and 3,136 emojis
numbers 0-9, letters A-Z,
a facsimile of the 46 Japanese characters
and all 50,000 Chinese ones,
plus a single abecedarian
incorporating every character, symbol and letter
from each of the other 20 or so mother tongues

a single pen stroke, guttural growl or subtle hand motion
from each of the 6,100 or so
living languages,
the dead ones too,
like Latin, Sanskrit and Old Norse,
fictional ones as well
like Klingon, Darthraki
and the Force

each seed is covered in cave paintings
and paintings of caves,
then blazed
with a soothsayer's prophetic raves,
sonically stuffed
with electromagnetic
micro
waves

once toasted, it's sun soaked
in ultraviolet rays
drenched in fountains of youth and old faithful,
submerged in Venezuela's Angel,
Canada's Horseshoe
and America's
Niagara
Falls

afterwords imbued with all alcohols--
isopropanol, methyl and ethyl,
dipped in butterscotch caramel,
double-chocolate,
red-velvet pretzel,
draped in silk, cotton, linen,
wool and satin fabric,
blessed by every priest, rabbi, minister,
reverend and bunny rabbit

it's face pict-o-grammed
with renderings of 1 million mountains
riveting razor ridges,
all person-made structures and bridges
along with a glimpse into every key text
from the world's most major religions--
plus of course their secondary sources,
like the seven valleys and the four,
holy bible, Torah and Quran, the vedas, to name a few
plus a list
of all lists,
both of those completed
and every to do

in essence it contains
a microscopic model of all galaxies
both known and yet to be known,
a multi-million membered mollusk cocktail
of all invertebrates and those with bones,
the preferred, neglected,
indifferent and highly favored,
the artificial and naturally flavored,
radioisotopes, stable and unstable,
and an inhalable, imbibable edible extraction
of all 118 elements on the periodic table

and so everyone reading this
and/or hearing this
is
an everything bagel

our families and our families families,
that which was aborted,
died shortly thereafter birth
and those carried to term,

the fresh, the pure,
the mold, the mildew, the germ,
really, everyone who ever was
and ever will be
is
an everything bagel
and a part of each and every
everything bagel.
which goes to say

there is only 1
truly everything bagel
it has
the grace of god,
the face of an atheist
and an agnostic's nose,
the scent of every flower,
every daisy every rose,
it's a big bang
of everything highly evolved and prehistoric,
all tangible things and the metaphoric,
the juvenile, the immature and sophomoric,
jam packed with the cat, the fiddle,
the cow and the moon,
the clean and dirty dishes,
the spoon and the- there is no spoon,

full of the virtual, the factual,
the abstract, the actual,
all harmonic frequencies
of the woodwinds, strings,
brass and piano keys,
a cacao cacophony of percussive instruments,
synthesizers and turntables

this everything bagel
whole in every way
contains all organs known to man
and even those only known
to aliens
respiratory, urinary and the endocrine,
digestive, muscular and integumentary --

like the skin,
reproductive, nervous and wait...
something
is
missing then

inside its complex circulatory system
of arteries , capillaries, PFO and veins
there lies pleasure, there lies, lies, pains,
there lies truths told and withheld claims

there lies cold feet,
lukewarm choices and old flames,
that which contains the container,
the outside the lines, front back and behind,
the tip of Everest
and floor of the Challenger Deep,
including every insomniac, every sleep,

the cool, calm collected and those prone to panic
the manic, satanic and addict giving up the drink
the attic, upstairs bathroom, living room and kitchen sink
the depressed, repressed and oppressed,
the bipolar, tripolar, and the polar express,
every helicopter, hot air balloon, every sub,
from the dirt on the ground to clouds high above,
blood, sweat, tears--
perhaps -
love

imprinted in all scents, smells, and fumes,
from Earth to Jupiter's moons
birth to tomb
from family vacation to romantic retreat,
tripping on acid
to tripping over
own two feet

all states, states of mind and entire nations
single stars and constellations,
a sign of all signs
zodiac,
stop and do not enter

this everything bagel
with that whole in the middle
is
kinda like my heart--
without its center,

this everything bagel
only one thing is missing from view
the whole of the middle,
like this hole in my heart
the hole that is missing,
is
you...

there once upon
was a time
when you were my everything
bagel
& i needed
nothing else
but now
i am
an everything bagel
& writing this has helped

so just as is with a poem about
truly
everything
i could never stop reading it
this everything bagel
i must never stop
eating it

never mind
the hole,
here it is, i refuse to hide it
the hole is only part of the whole
i still have a heart
and here
is
what's inside it.

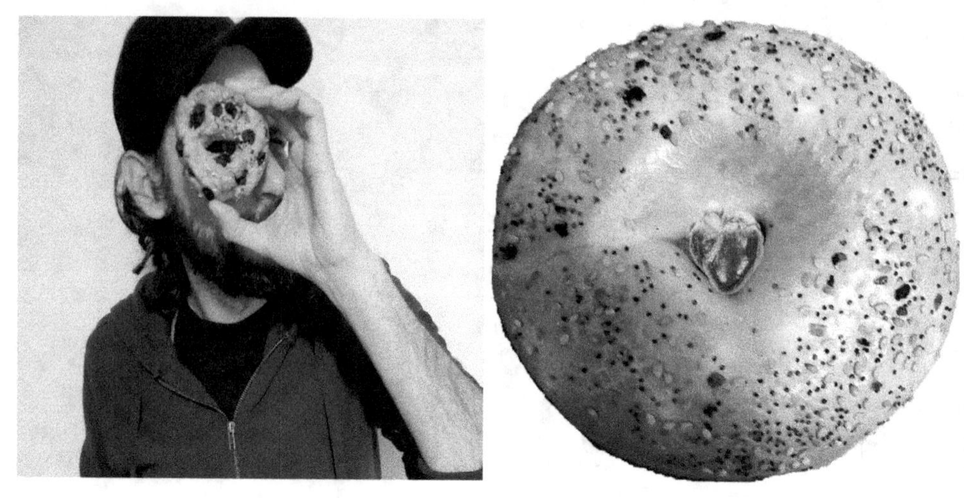

2. Everything In My Heart

those who truly lived and died that i knew most personally, family
and friends who reached their untimely end,

at the time of this writing, December 31st, 2020 i hold these,
the forest five of an extended family tree,
forever in my heart with love, taken too soon
Grandpa Lewis Raven, Grandma Rosalie Raven,
Mother Bonnie C. Raven Tarazevits,
Dear Friend Allan Weingarden and Aunt Zelma Weinberg

i by no means wish to exclude all others who i love
who are still living,
eternally grateful for their presence in my life,
especially during this most difficult year
for so many
nor do I wish to leave out those countless others
who have died i still think kindly on

so to conclude i have also included
eulogy poems that i wrote and delivered
for two of the aforementioned deceased
and their loved ones
and a few words for other names in mind
i was able
of those in my heart
missing from my everything bagel.

3. Grandpa Lewis M. Raven, 4/05/1994

of a cerebral hemorrhage, who would bring over half the *fixins bar* from a Roy Rogers rest stop, replete with pickles and slaw. A decorated health inspector who paved the way for my brother's profession, always put a premium on eating salads and fruit. There wasn't a watermelon season he'd miss, no cantaloupe or honeydew could sneak past him. I can easily attribute to him a healthy relationship to food, especially when acquired free of charge and his love for my grandmother was visibly so. His hair slicked back and shiny well into his 80's, his ears believe it or not bigger than mine, looked like tiny Ewoks gripping the side of his head. I never knew he was born in Germany until recently, which is odd considering his wife and daughter always audibly rooted for the Jewish contestants and against the German sounding names on all the game shows. Lewis later lived in Newark before moving to Edison, just a hop and a skip from Menlo Park Mall, back when the decor was orange and black, and neither food courts nor cell phone kiosks existed. He served as the prez of the Philly Conference of Food, Drug and Health Officials and vice of the NJ Association of Sanitarians. Like me, he graduated from Rutgers, where he was instrumental in the creation of Helyar House which to this day still provides affordable housing for Cook Campus Students. Unconditionally loved, a sanitarian of supreme mastery, I can still see his hands flashing the okay sign and how he impacted me so satisfactorily.

4. My Mother, Bonnie C. Raven-Tarazevits, 12/20/1995

cancer of the lung, that spread everywhere else, was born in Atlantic City, taught first grade in Dunellen, NJ where she met my jump roping dad. She went on to become a dedicated ESL teacher, her pupils an honorary extension of her own flesh and blood. Her thick, reddish-brown tresses didn't make it to the mud, radioactively nudged, yet upon her passing, her grieving students wrote letters to my family in a language she had taught them to master, comforting, heartfelt letters that might not have existed if not for her. My first audience, before she got sick I'd perform at the foot of her bed as she cackled at my Yankovic. I believed she was Miss America, although she wasn't, she coulda been a Jeopardy contender, a grandmother, a phone call away among so many other things and I still see her in the mirror and occasionally backstage waiting with wings in the wings.

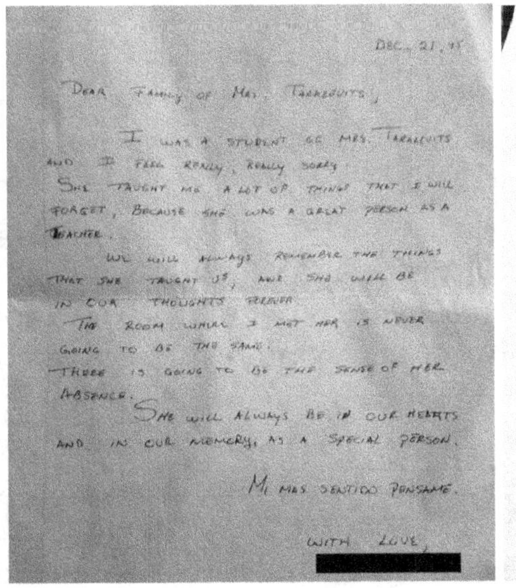

DEC. 21, 95

Dear Family of Mrs. Tarazevits,

I was a student of Mrs. Tarazevits and I feel really, really sorry. She taught me a lot of things that I will forget, because she was a great person as a teacher.

We will always remember the things that she taught us, and she will be in our thoughts forever.

The room where I met her is never going to be the same.

There is going to be the sense of her absence.

She will always be in our hearts and in our memory, as a special person.

Mi mas sentido pensame.

With love,

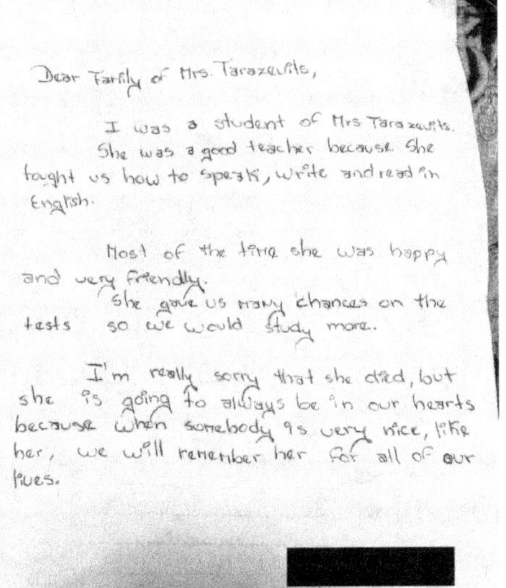

Dear Family of Mrs. Tarazevits,

I was a student of Mrs Tarazevits. She was a good teacher because she taught us how to speak, write and read in English.

Most of the time she was happy and very friendly.

She gave us many chances on the tests so we would study more.

I'm really sorry that she died, but she is going to always be in our hearts because when somebody is very nice, like her, we will remember her for all of our lives.

5. Grandma Rosalie Simon-Raven, 1/19/2000

of Minsk, Russia lived 19 days past the supposed y2K, dying in January of 2000, although both of our worlds came crashing down 5 years before when she had to bury her own child. All eyes wet, shoveling dirt on her gravestone, my north star headed south, grandma was visibly upset. Even with both compasses now passed, I still feel closer to Grandma Rosalie than any woman I've ever met, even those I've yet to meet. She was the first person to understand me without having to speak. I'd spend countless hours by her side, holding her hand on the couch. Although wrinkly, her skin was smoother than reverse sandpaper and she'd often note how good my circulation was as a measure of nothing else but the pinkness of my nails. There was talk she made bombs, was a trackstar and was quite the writer. She's the only one in the family who took the time to write thoughtful messages on cards for special occasions. I responded in kind with compliments, patience and kindness to her always. Of course my love and hers were given freely although she'd sometimes slip me 100 dollar bills. I think that could be why I often rely on women to find me jobs and have had a string of female bosses, platonically paying them with hardwork and a smile. Rosalie at first objected to me dating a gentile, for no other reason than her Catholic name, but 180'd around to full acceptance of a love for whoever I damn well pleased. In retrospect, she might have been protecting me from unsuspecting heartbreak, for somehow she must have sensed the girl in question's affections were wholly unrequited. Often floral scented, with an acerbic wit with whomever she would meet, Rosalie by any other name would still smell as sweet, an observer who downplayed how much she knew, who's influence echoes in almost everything I do.

Lewis and Rosalie styling and smiling on the AC Boardwalk

6. Allan Winegarden Friend, Of Cancer, 10/25/2004

was a brother and a stepbrother, died childless but much like a father, a guardian angel and a friend of no familial relation. I went to Hebrew School and high-school with him where I minimized him as being highly intelligent and devotedly Jewish, which he was, but so much more. In college we pledged together and became fraternity brothers, where he taught me things about money and business that my dad knew nothing about. Last time I saw him we literally broke breadsticks, shared unlimited soups and salads at an Olive Garden with friends who've always felt like family. Who knew, weeks later he'd be slipped into the soil, implanted in my memory, and I'd have a chance to wax on wax off (poetically) to a Miyagi-like mentor, in a funeral eulogy on his never-ending influence.

In Loving Memory Of Allan Winegarden
recited at his funeral service for family, friends
& brothers of Sigma Chi's Iota Psi Chapter

Allan Wine-Garden of Eden- first *real* man I ever met,
yet death swept in before his 25th and regrettably
for his last few moments I wasn't with.
But while he lived this man was more than myth,
and more than meets the eye,
transformed me from naïve boy to hard-nosed guy
to bleeding blue and gold with Sigma-Sigma Chi.

He was more than a brother, he was more like a father.
An honorable man behind the glass, that was never a bother,
embodying ideals behind shields
that wielded more magic than Harry Potter.
Days spent with Allan were more refreshing
than a crisp cool glass of ice water.
Big Al as he was affectionately known, slimmed down to suaveness
with muscles more toned than a Sylvester Stallone clone.
Compassionate, nurturing and always willing
to lend a helping standing ovation,
he was more than on track, this *Champ* was the whole station

He was more than a father he was more like a teacher,
a master class math wiz, every relationship of his
was more balanced than equations on a trig quiz.
I learned more from him than most of my professors.
Always giving his all, never no lesser, a sharp dresser,
always had the answers, never a guesser,
knew all about the stock market, weightlifting and nutrition,
knowledge that ranged from business to finance
all the way back to fly-fishing.

He was more than a teacher, he was more like an angel.
He had a heart bigger than a shopping cart
with a diamond studded finish,
a friend forever with a stronger-will
than Popeye eating fifteen cans of spinach.
A preceptor with ceptor a king of the dorms,
busting kids for weed, yet comforting them through storms.
A USY Basketball state champion two years consecutive on the courts-
A force on the boards and a master of horse,
he could box out better than quadrilaterals in a geometry course.

We pledged together in '99
and spent more time puzzled than you'd believe
that gave way to absurd nicknames to grin while we grieve,
Ichabod, Barf, Buckwheat the Beave,
Webster, Newman, there was also Tinky-Winky- but he had to leave.
Together we found Runkle, Lockwood, Jordan and Cooper,
Caldwell, Scobey and Bell.

Wherever he may be
I wish him more well than swells of wishing wells
beside a fantastical genie,
transmitting the simple words DREAM ME
to help comfort all friends and family "who can no longer see me."
In our hearts and in our heads, for all eternity.
Granting him the utmost peace, love and serenity.

7. Zelma Weinberg, Aunt, Of Cancer, 4/04/06

could type more words per minute than a stenographer on amphetamines and played a mean game of Free-cell. Her memory was sublime, she knew more about someone's day than they did, with an attention to detail any editor would admire. Her secretarial skills unmatched, two amazing kids and a happy go lucky husband with mysterious travel tales I was only beginning to absorb. Aunt Zel had an ornate and trippy rug of which I was known to obsessively play with its tassels, an antennaed TV from the stone age and a barely sat upon couch wrapped in plastic, surrounded by elephant figurines. She brunched with her gal pals long before it was trendy and cool, helped me with school and she felt exactly like what an aunt should be.

still hear their voices, speak to their stones and in mirrors see.
gone but not forgotten 3 matriarchs of me (l to r. mom aunt grandma)

Eulogy Poem For Aunt Zelma Weinberg
Died March 4, 2006 delivered once at her funeral service two days after

If blisters twist your innards and you miss her...
I know now we have the reunion of two sisters.

Last time we spoke, we watched *Dancing With The Stars*...
Well, Zel is now dancing 'in' the stars,
sitting at a blackjack table beside the bar
watching *Game Show Network* to the left of Mars.
And I'm sure she'll continue to fax from afar,
double-spaced and spell-checked
forever into our dreams and emotional tip-jar
her life-changing, always impactful
memoirs...

A better secretary than most,
she'd also type up college essays and notes,
co-workers would boast
she wrapped around every task like winding magic rope.
And you can be sure her ghost will be front and center at Macy's
resuming her shopping post,
a quality holiday dinner host, who'd never *pass-over*
a solid pot roast
and as far as food goes,
she'll be missed by every chain restaurant on the East Coast.

They say ants ruin picnics, but with Zel every visit became a picnic.
Great discussions that will stick with me for many years to come,
Like a pack of flavorful, smile-inducing chewing gum.
If I arrived with a box of candy and a bag of chips
I'd often leave with a turkey dinner,
some apple juice and nacho cheese dip.
So long as I didn't mention any form of butter or she'd flutter away,
keeping the mustard, sour cream and mayonnaise OFF of her tray.

Her heart was bigger than Showboat,
Tropicana and the Trump Towers combined,

I never met a better listener,
she knew my schedule better than I knew mine.
Her kindness spread more than what caused her decline
and her genuine concern for all people was never out of line...
always asking, "What's the matter!" even when things were fine.

She was one of the few people I've known who cried
as much out of happiness
as she did out of grief.
Her tears could be beautiful,
putting warmongers to peace.
and crying babies to sleep.
Not to mention,
she helped raise two of the best kids you'll ever meet
who each have growing families of their own
with amazing grandchildren she talked to more than ET phoned home.
Never skipping her rock-hard friendships
made of diamond-studded stone,
she was also a caring wife to a korean war vet husband
who never picked a bone.

So, if blisters twist your innards and you too miss her...
know now we have the reunion of two sisters-
beside a mother doing a crossword puzzle with a cup of rice pudding,
while watching *Wheel of Fortune* each and every single day,
and a father feasting on watermelon and some Roy Roger's salad bar
flashing with love from above
Yaaa...we're o-kay!!

8. Y Love

yes i feel blessed in many ways on most days
to have such a caring and compassionate Den,
she thinks deeply and sleeps softy
i'm tea and she's coffee
we fight a little,
often over subtleties such as these,
a disconnect between her science and my art
even though it's bigger than that
or not as big
i can't always tell the difference

i like that she likes sunflowers, sunsets,
cats and ice-rinks
she doesn't like that i don't like to drink
she certainly works more than 40 winks
yet we seem to be working out the kinks

i think she thinks of others a lot
we may have started similarly
but is a great deal of what i'm not
i like when we read together on off days
we're working on getting and staying same page

i think she speaks and acts practically
reacts emotionally and empathically,
yet always ethically
i think practically,
react, act and emotionally cope-
poetically

is how much stock i plop in words
is as pathetic a poetic fallacy
there can be,
why, when i am happy as a clam

to live in my surreality?
love her, i do
very much - there's no one else
but have trouble during the moments
when she doesn't love herself

she reminds me of my grandmother, my aunt,
my mother
rolled into one familial toke
more anxious than my mom,
maybe because she doesn't smoke
she has trouble taking
but not making a joke
she looks amazing in dresses
that don't even cost much
and will hike, bike and run for miles by your side
even when out of steam

courtship online over *the Wheel* and Pat
who knew i'd get so close to her and Vanna, her cat
she beat me in basketball on our first date
i'd want her on my every team
i sure didn't play fair for the next three years
and made a nightmare out a Caribbean dream
since showed support
so proud of her accomplishments
even though i may have altered her course
before she entered the picture
let everything else be a blur
who knows what else might occur

in our feature length movie
she wins best DOC
although so many don't get to see it
from scrubs to her lab coat of arms

she helps heal with feeling those who need it
med-ucating many including me

a rocky start
though when we end up hiking
bear, beacon the grand canyon and beyond
she climbs into my heart and we bond

stood by ever since
what we lack matches
together a whole hole
of bandaged patches
sensibly doesn't make much sense,
but our everything bagels are missing the same contents.

9. Love 4 All

i heart those who are lonely
those together who are also lonely,
those terribly sick and newly injured
i feel scared and anxious on some days
running, writing, painting helps
i'm usually good at getting myself out of a funk
i've been staying in them for far shorter periods
which is good
less of a mess
although i occasionally play chess,
Scrabble or Tetris too long,
most days i'm not doing anything destructive,
but it's not constructive either…or is it
to simply sit there, in silence, sometimes in the dark…
my mind isn't racing, my hearts beating,
i'm breathing, i'm just being
doing
nothing
i can do anything
but you can't do everything
i heart all creators of art
both the critically acclaimed and inane
those with ideas expressed and those yet to start
the haves have nots rich broke and broken
all who i've spoken and yet to speak to
who've let go to keep going and grew.

10. Lost Loves That Are Without A Doubt Not Sonnets

1
of all the women i have been with i dream of one the most
and i don't know if this is because
she was the woman OF my dreams
or there's some unfinished business between us
or more likely because she has always been
such a big dreamer herself,
the sheer magnitude of her dreams
finds their way into all other people's dreams
it's an ingredient that makes for a great artist
and i am excited for what she's doing and she's done.

2
after a play-reading of the Crucible
i double backed for her number
our first conversation was about health insurance
over a burger and fries
courting over email
then pad thai and banana pancakes
by bridge over River Kwais
Mike Myers live and the Irish countryside
we were almost married
to our Central Park apartment
free trips to Jamaica and Florida every Christmas
i thought she had anger issues
hell, i'd a been angry too
both for what i did and didn't do
now we check in on holidays
meet every now and again for pizza
last time we hung out she picked me up
from a rental car place that wouldn't give me a car
i helped her move a dresser
then used *her* car

to drive to my cousins in Jersey and do my taxes
i bought her a burrito on my way back
and on her way dropping me off by a train
she showed me a good place she likes to watch sunsets
with her boyfriend
all i want for her now
is everything she wants
without me in the picture
even though
she's in so many memorable ones
of mine.

3
how to think about and frame
all the could have beens or might have worked
the nameless and the named
the at first sighted, overlooked, the timing was a little off
the started to fall, but got caught up
the unrequited on the other side
the ships that sailed, the missed your chance,
the perfect match that caught flame fast
that burned up bad
and didn't last.

3.
the friends who went on to marry
some to carry child others career
still near and dear to my heart
others single still
who's companionship has meant the world
who alone together
we created art
and conversations worth a canvas
those who've soothed, amused and moved
that i so dearly miss.

11. My Miss America

I was always told and always believed that my mother was Miss America. I saw no crown, I saw no sash but she was beautiful to many and most beautiful to me and that's all I needed, that was enough, yet I never stopped to think about what's the stuff that makes a good Miss America both then and now and what that figure has come to represent amongst us, them and W.O.W.

As a child all it took was a wicked smile, hot bod and one of a kind looks to say the least, then as a teen, it was a congenial bent, sexy swimsuit and wishing for world peace. Forgive the mans-plane coming in for the landing, but nowadays, I think it's silly to suggest 1 woman can represent the entirety of a state, a country, a universe when there's so much incredible diversity of thought, body and representation.* My Miss America's no doubt different from his, hers, theirs, them's, yours, so who could possibly decide, nevertheless, I still occasionally go along for the ride.

The first Miss America was Model Margaret Gorman, out of D.C. - winner of the Golden Mermaid Trophy by way of seaside ceremony in Atlantic City, same place my mother was born just 23 years before, while the most recent Miss A, Camile Shrier on the count of Corona has now held the title two years running, arriving on the scene on DeCember 19 - nineteen.

So somewhere between a flawless floor routine and falling off the balance beam lies the talented and talentless, where these Queens to be have given their best. Miss America's have sung, danced and roller skated into our hearts- ventriloquy-ed, soliloquy-ed and traipsed on jagged glass; even mixed chemicals into 3 separate flasks. I wonder what mom would have done - inspired students in an ESL class? Blew bubbles, twirled cigarettes, made matzo ball soup, laughed?

Sure I'd like to see a Miss America juggle a job, family and kids while ripping a poem underwater in a puppy press handstand or meditating on a mountain performing open heart(s) surgery on an octopus, but doesn't this take the same near impossible beauty standards and just switch them for a set of damn near unattainable special skills?

I celebrate all those women who spin so many plates, straddling anxieties, depression and fears amidst the blood sweat and tears, raising glass ceilings into the stratosphere.

But perhaps there should be other categories? Like ethics, an empathy check, athletics, accounting and business IQ. Fundraising, child rearing and charity 101 with double the cash prize to lessen the wage gap, although the winner is given a 50k scholarship and a six figure contract.

The first Miss America's had to be unmarried and white, and their choices were slight, unallowed to have an abortion with no kids in site. And aside from mindless misogyny, hijacked flights, conspiracy theorists and racist fights, the main things I'd like to miss - America are new viruses, missiles and meteorites.

At the time of her death at 51, my mom still could have competed in the "Ms." America pageant, which honors those who've at least hit the half century mark, but she missed Miss America by more than a quarter as today contestants must be between 17 and 25, childless, with their health in working order.

My mother, even though out of New Jersey repped a particular state of mind- to be kind always, thoughtful and hardworking, intelligent, compassionate and patient- she was an American dream of mine, and at least to me, I suppose a fine representation of this flawed yet distinctly beautiful nation.

So to close, whether she was or wasn't, Most of the time, I sure do miss...America.

My Miss America, Miss Bonnie Raven's Teacher ID

*Although slowly becoming somewhat more inclusive, there are many separate pageants in this country and abroad, including one's for Miss Black USA, Miss Teen USA, Miss Trans Star International, Miss Earth, Miss World, Miss Arab USA, Miss Asia, Miss Native American USA, Miss Hawaiian Tropic, Miss Supetalent, etc.

Miss America no longer has a swimsuit competition, but Miss USA does.

Miss United States of America bans trans women from competing, but this is different from Miss USA and Miss Universe which do not.

First trans-woman to compete in Miss Universe was Angela Ponce in 2018.

Miss USA goes on to compete in Miss Universe.

12. Strides and Staircases

An acrostic Sconnettt for LC, my dad's new wife
who has in heart and help extended his dear life

Not crossing gaps you're defeated from start
Our unseated queen's replaced with new face,
This fall down stairs impairs one's beating heart,
So take baby steps in making true space,
One step forward, one step...closer, embrace.
Enabling in-laws might stunt real progress,
Voice concerns early and try and have faith
If not 12 steps just take one to accept.
Let fairy god mother's breathe the cool breeze
Stepmoms are not always out to deceive
The way Cinderella had us believe
Eventually defense mechs will bleed.
Placing blood with non blood's still sorta blood,
Sure you might not look alike, but there's love.

13. Reyla B. Glick

my JP Stevens High School drama teacher of a deadly virus, May 23, 1997.

She taught me to act. It was the first class I was treated like and talked to as an adult, yet where I learned how to be a kid at heart always. She challenged us all to be better and brighter, her class and backstage couch was the safest of spaces, yet always where provocative and dangerous conversations took place, she instilled and willed every thespian with an emotional life raft along with a lifelong love and appreciation for the craft. She appreciated my shyness offstage and my subtlety on, I grew more bombastic when she was gone. From Simon to Shanley, Arthur Miller to Medoff, death of an incredible instructor, somewhere in the deep blue sea of a brightened beach memory. Every session was a masterclass in life itself. I'd freeze tag time back then if it would help, and ask advice, play the question game, IMPROV medicine or hear her laugh. I'd have easily ended up in an acting conservatory, if she hadn't passed, yet think of all the actors she did make, instead I found poetry, which has allowed me to candle write this wake, yet still bring her with me onto every stage I take.

14. Albert Baron Solomon

aka Doctor SilliMilliMum born of another world, died in the Philippines, October 27, 2019.

somewhere between a silly senility and genuine genius
"employees must wash hands"
the dirtiest, clean metaphysical comic
was a one man band - of bizarre,
bright as a light but
two points shy of a star
who'd leave impromptu songs on my voicemail,
that always made me smile
substituting rhythm for gism, and squirrel for squirt
his Brando and Julia Child were wild
blurting out inappropriate words and phases
he always got us giggling, if you went along for the ride
he was lovingly loopy, human nitrous oxide
married twice, worked as a transcriptionist for thirty
lots of his early life was a mystery
old as time- yet gone too soon
i took him out for thai food once and i almost moved
into his apartment's spare room.
i was invited to lunch at his house and hesitantly obliged
not knowing what i'd find inside,
he kept bones and eggshells in his pots,
we ate omelets, made bacon and drank OJ
beside every document, obscure file and tchotchke
he ever received in his Havishamesque
living room. I was supposed to take him to the airport
the day he left, but we got the date wrong
and I never saw him after that,
but amidst the tears when i think on him, i laugh.

15. The 18 beautiful souls I interviewed on **The Good Grief Podcast** and their lost loved ones.*

1.   Mother of Matt
2.   Mother of Kyle
3.   Mother of Omar
4.   Mother of Yarden
5.   Mother of Bob
6.   Mother of Ina
7.   Mother of Jenny
8.   Mother of Justin
9.   Mother of Dorianne
10. Father of Josh
11. Father of Jacob
12. Father of Maya
13. Father of Malcolm
14. Mother and Father of Anne
15. Mother and Father of Nicole
16. Mother and Father of Miles
17. Mother and Father of Joel
18. Father of my Father

*Visit TheGoodGriefPodcast.com for more.

16. Polygon To Get A Bagel

My theory of everything bagels may be the center of my universe
but flagels out to fall flat with regards to
the gravitational pull of an impending wedding

just as this Michael Baygel explodes with flavor,
slowly transforming into a tiny car,
traversing my bacteria-harboring, once pearly whites
as if Armageddon.

Garlic bagels make my vampire interactions more memorable
and my kisses more ephemeral.
A tall poppy seed bagel
is no better than a donut hole
with just as many carbs,
and as for these ass-whole-wheat bagels,
I'd rather starve.

This pumpernickel-back bagel reminds me of nice crap,
while this Cinnamon raisins, raisin' hell at the spice rack.
Assault bagels usually get thrown out
while this pretzel bagel twists and shouts.

The sunflower bagel will come out tomorrow
to a reading rainbow bagel before the show
so long as the french toast bagel proposes
the asiago bagel
kills Emilia and not Othello.

This sesame street bagel is brought to you by
green jello, number two and the letter o
while the blueberry bagel
is buried in the snow.

17. The Impossibility Of Nothing

by embryo
there is
something
a fetus something more
once out there is no turning back
cord is cut but we record

every moment in our brains
attached to bodies
we barely need,
only when we die
is there nothing but the essence of you
in all that you'll conceive

and a sense that
you existed
by all who thought
they knew you did
for however long
you lasted

before me there was you and before you there was them
but before them there was this and that
and before matter there was space
as a matter
of fact

or fiction depending on who you ask
big bang and then *voila*, we appear
or a mirrorverse upon which time adheres
everything and all possibilities have already occurred
and now we play in reverse until big bang the third

and so forth until five six seven eight on its side

as for me
post embryo
i'm pushing past forty

still haven't found Nemo
finding Dory
and the Nothing
is just an antagonizing force
in a
Neverending Story

The Know Nothings knew what they were not
my mistress' i's are nothing but puns
and when i am nothing
am i still Scott?

i am nothing
or no thing
do you know things
i know a thing or two
ain't no thing
but a *g-h-i-j-k-l-m-n-o* thing
a Dr. No thing
no thing is too small no thing is too big
no thingamabob thingamajig
no no thing
noh thing
yes or no thing
know it all thing
no thing to see here
nothing appears in the rear
no thing
no
n
.

18. Eighteen Edgars Part 3*

As I stare at my mom's headstone, I pick-up the phone hoping it's her. It's not. On the other end is a casting director for a show I've worked on before, asking if I can stand in again for the host. I'm not exactly sure what to say in this case, like, "I'm so sorry, I can't, my mom died…18 years ago," or "I wish I could, but I'm kind of at a cemetery right now." Instead I tell them I'm visiting family in New Jersey and will be there in less than 2 hours. They say get there when you can, so I sob a bit before heading back to the rental car. Annnd- it won't start. O, the irony of a dead battery while visiting a gravesite. But it's still so early and I swear I didn't even use the lights. Either way, something or someone is keeping me here and I'm due on the set of *Brain Games* in under an hour. And believe me I need the money, like I need a new car, like I need a get out of debt free card, like I needed this cry-atholon, like I need…a mom.

Truthfully, there's no place I'd rather be right now than here with my mother, maybe with the exception of a stage, acting in some capacity, performing my heart out for all to see both behind or in front of a camera, recreating reality. So I call them back informing them of my car trouble, asking if it's okay to get there after lunch, not even hinting-at-in-the-slightest to the possible supernatural forces tethering me to this sacred spot. Apparently, there's been a water main break on set and arriving after 1 will be fine. I continue fiddling with the car to no avail. I check the trunk. Why? I'm not exactly sure. It's not like a spare tire is going to help me in this case, or a jack- but perhaps some magic seeds and a beanstalk might, inching me closer to heaven in the sky, a golden goose, a giant's eye. I mean, what else am I hoping to find? I swear there are no bodies back there, besides there are plenty surrounding my car already and I'm in no mood to dig. I get back in the driver's seat and take a moment to sit with the spirits.

The remains of most of my family are less than 50 yards apart, so it's easy to imagine them all in the car. Grandpa's in the front insisting we all remain calm, making sure all is up to code. My grandmother's in the middle. I remember hearing stories that she once fell out of the car while it was moving and I'd hate to have that happen again, even if she's already dead. My aunt is positioned passenger right looking out the window, proofreading everything written on the gravestones outside the glass, asking what's the matter, when some leaves hit the roof and we laugh. Mom's behind me with the left window cracked in case she wants to light up a cigarette. You've heard the old adage, it's not polite to breathe in front of those who can't, well it's not polite to smoke in front of them either, so she chews some gum instead, reverse popping bubbles in her mouth, suggesting we play a word game to pass the time.

I'm going on a trip and I'm bringing my dead mother, my long gone grandfather, my deceased grandmother and my decomposing aunt.

I realize I never had a chance to drive my mom - anywhere, even though she took me to so many places herself - Hebrew School and Bar Mitzvah lessons, friend's houses. She even chaperoned my first date to miniature golf and TCBY yogurt. Perhaps if I press hard enough on the gas, I can transport my family not only out of this cemetery, but go back to the future, freeing them from their final resting place, wherever it might be. But they are at peace, while this car is stalled. My career is stalled. My relationship has stalled. *I am stalled..*

I call the company I rented from, it's one of those ride shares you pick up from a garage using an access card and a passcode. Apparently I was given the wrong car and the company shut off the engine because they can do that sort of thing whenever they want. A perfectly rational explanation, but I see it as a sort of sign. Me inside the wrong car I take as me being in the wrong relationship. I'm on the wrong path. I drop off the wrong car and still manage to make it to the set on time, where I'm promptly painted in polka dots.*** Not only am I standing in for the host, but I'm part of an optical illusion for the day tasked with blending in to a background, only to jump out and seemingly appear from out of nowhere. Make of that what you will, but a few weeks later my engagement is called off, I move out of the apartment we share and we go our separate ways. ** And for a while I'm in a somewhat better place. I deepen my friendships. I travel. I grieve. I tour. I write. And I eventually meet someone new. Almost too soon I meet someone new and it takes me until now to write this as she soundly sleeps next to me, a whopping eight years since I made that trip. I'm thinking of going back, but this time I have someone interested and emotionally invested in coming with. You see she has someone special underneath the peat - lying supine in the same cemetery as mine is Margalite, her pearl of a mother, which begs the question, do you think they know each other?

I to r, a row of Ravens reverberating from the good place
Mom Grandpa Aunt and Grandma
facing us in warm embrace

*Part 1 and 2 appear as separate audio poems in *A to N - of Words, Part 1* and *A to N - of Words, Bonus Tracks*, respectively. Both parts were also published as one in print in the Late Orphan Anthology's, *These Summer Months*. This is the 1st and only printing of Part 3.

**See 10. (4) for more context and *I'm Not Michael Phelps* on A to N of Words.

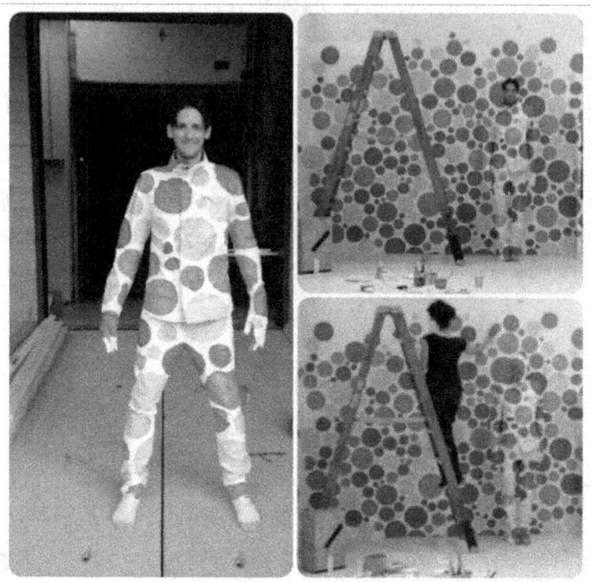

***on set and off, where in the wall-dough-style painted in polka dots

About The Author's Eating Habits

Scott Raven Tarazevits has an aversion to sour cream and mayonnaise. He occasionally breaks out into hives, most often after consuming bbq sauce then running. He won't eat a cheeseburger, but would have a grilled cheese sandwich then a steak had he not become a pescetarian in 2018. He loves lobster, pizza, bhel puri, and smoothies. He also loves everything bagels and wants to know what's on yours? Submit a short poem outlining what's on your everything bagel to scotttraven@gmail.com for a chance to win $88 and publication in an upcoming issue of *ninecloud journal*.org. Check out more of Scottt's work at: *thegoodgriefpodcast.com*, with *Mayhem Poets* and the upcoming, *Forest Hills Plantdemic*.

www.ingramcontent.com/pod-product-compliance
Lightning Source LLC
Chambersburg PA
CBHW050708250726

48662CB00002B/901